PRAYER & STUDY

STORMIE OMARTIAN

LEAD ME, HOLY SPIRIT

HARVEST HOUSE PUBLISHERS
EUGENE, OREGON

Cover by Koechel Peterson & Associates, Inc., Minneapolis, Minnesota

Back cover author photo © Harry Langdon

LEAD ME, HOLY SPIRIT PRAYER AND STUDY GUIDE
Copyright © 2012 by Stormie Omartian
Published by Harvest House Publishers
Eugene, Oregon 97402
www.harvesthousepublishers.com

ISBN 978-0-7369-4777-0 (pbk.)
ISBN 978-0-7369-4778-0 (eBook)

Printed in the United States of America

12 13 14 15 16 17 18 19 20 / LB-SK / 10 9 8 7 6 5 4 3 2 1

This book belongs to

_____

Please do not read beyond this page
without permission of the person named above.

A supplemental workbook to

Lead Me, Holy Spirit

by Stormie Omartian

Contents

———

‰ ‹

What You Should
Know Before You Begin

———

Welcome to a study about following the leading of the Holy Spirit. This *Prayer and Study Guide* is designed to help you have a closer relationship with God, receive all that Jesus has for you, and learn to hear God speaking to your heart. Responding to the questions and suggestions in each chapter will strengthen your understanding of who God is, what Jesus has done for you, and all the Holy Spirit wants to do in your life.

What You Need in Order to Begin

This is a 12-week plan, but you can double up the chapters and do it in six weeks if you desire. Or, if you are not in a group, you can go at your own pace and do as much as you want whenever you like.

In order to go through the study, you will need my book *Lead Me, Holy Spirit* (from now on referred to as "the book") and your Bible. I have used the New King James Version here, but you can use any translation you like. It would be good to have a small notebook or journal with you so you can write down whatever God speaks to your heart as you read His Word and pray. And don't forget a pen or pencil.

When Doing This Study in a Group

If you are doing this *Prayer and Study Guide* in a group, read the chapter or chapters assigned that week from the book and then answer the corresponding questions in this study guide. Each time the group meets, the leader will go over the questions and encourage members to share their answers or any insights they have received from the Lord while doing the study. Because some of the questions are personal, don't feel you must say anything you are not comfortable sharing with the group. On the other hand, feel free to be transparent about your own personal experiences whenever you feel led by the Spirit to do so. Your freedom to share can release others who are hesitant. Your experiences in following the leading of the Holy Spirit will be a great personal encouragement for everyone else.

The answers to Bible-based questions are always good to share with one another, however, so don't hesitate to contribute whatever you have learned, discovered, or experienced that would be beneficial for others to hear.

Pray the prayer together at the end of each chapter in the book as a starting point from which people are led to pray for one another about the things that concern them.

Ask God to Give You a New and Fresh Perspective

When you are asked in this *Prayer and Study Guide* to write out your prayers, know that just as spoken prayers are powerful, so are written prayers. And these written prayers will not only help you focus on what to pray about, but they will also facilitate your developing a richer prayer life. As you become more at ease communicating with the Lord in an ongoing way, you will find it easier to hear the Holy Spirit speaking to your heart.

→ ←

Week One

Read: "What Does It Mean to Be Led by the Holy Spirit"
and Chapter 1: "Led to Receive"
in LEAD ME, HOLY SPIRIT

Led to Receive the Relationship with God You Have Always Needed

1. Read John 6:47-51. What does Jesus refer to Himself as and why?

_____

_____

_____

_____

_____

What is the bread Jesus is talking about, and what happens when you partake of it?

_____

_____

_____

_____

_____

What do you have when you receive Jesus?

_____

_____

_____

_____

2. Read John 6:40. What is God's will concerning Jesus?

_____

_____

_____

_____

What is God's will and His promise for you regarding Jesus?

_____

_____

_____

_____

_____

3. Read Romans 5:8-10. What did God demonstrate to you by sending His Son, Jesus, to die for you?

_____

_____

_____

_____

What did Jesus' death accomplish for you?

_____

_____

_____

_____

4. Read John 3:5. What did Jesus say you have to do to enter the king-dom of God?

_____

_____

_____

_____

Read Acts 2:38. What do you have to do in order to receive the Holy Spirit?

_____

_____

_____

_____

5. Read Philippians 2:8-10. What did Jesus do for us?

_____

_____

_____

_____

_____

What did God do for Jesus?

_____

_____

_____

_____

What should we do in response to the name of Jesus?

_____

_____

_____

_____

6. Read 1 Corinthians 12:3. If you are being led by the Holy Spirit, what could you never do?

_____

_____

_____

_____

If someone is unable to say that Jesus is Lord of their life, what does that indicate?

_____

_____

_____

_____

_____

Have you declared Jesus to be Lord of your life? If your answer is yes, write out a prayer thanking Him for what He has done by saving you. If your answer is no, write out a prayer asking Him to come into your life and forgive you of all past sins and to lead you into the life He has for you as your Savior and Deliverer.

_____

_____

_____

_____

⊶⊷

PRAY THE PRAYER ON PAGES 22-23 IN THE BOOK.

Led to Receive the Promise of God's Spirit in You

7. Read Luke 11:11-13. Describe how much God wants you to have the Holy Spirit.

_____

_____

_____

_____

If we already have the Holy Spirit when we repent and are baptized in water (Acts 2:38), why do we need to ask God for the Holy Spirit? (Read page 26, second paragraph, in the book.)

_____

_____

_____

8. Read Luke 4:18. Jesus read this Scripture from the Old Testament in the synagogue and said it was now fulfilled in Him. In your own words, what did Jesus accomplish because the Spirit of the Lord was upon Him?

_____

_____

_____

_____

_____

9. Read Isaiah 61:1-3. Of all the acts Jesus did because the Spirit of the Lord was upon Him, which ones are you thankful for right at this moment? Write out your answer as a prayer to the Lord. (For example, "Lord, I am so thankful You are my comfort in a time of mourning...")

_____

_____

_____

_____

_____

10. Read Romans 8:9-11. Complete the following sentences:

You are in the Spirit if_____

_____

_____

_____

If you do not have the Holy Spirit, then you are not _____

_____

_____

_____

_____

If the Spirit of God, who raised Jesus from the dead, is in you, what will happen when you die?

_____

_____

_____

_____

Read Romans 8:16. In light of this Scripture, what is your inheritance because you have received Jesus and have the Holy Spirit in you?

_____

_____

_____

11. Read John 14:26. By what name did Jesus refer to the Holy Spirit?

_____

_____

_____

_____

What did Jesus promise regarding the Holy Spirit?

_____

_____

_____

_____

_____

Read John 16:7-9. Why did Jesus have to be crucified and go to heaven?

_____

_____

_____

_____

What did Jesus say the Holy Spirit—the Helper—would do when He came?

_____

_____

_____

_____

_____

PRAY THE PRAYER ON PAGES 27-28 IN THE BOOK.

Led to Receive the Freedom and Wholeness God Has for You

12. Read Ephesians 3:20. What is God able to do in our lives and why?

_____

_____

_____

_____

13. Read 2 Corinthians 3:17. What is the most important thing you need in your life in order to find the freedom and wholeness God has for you?

_____

_____

_____

_____

14. Read John 10:10. What does the enemy want to do in your life?

_____

_____

_____

What does Jesus want to do?

_____

_____

_____

With regard to finding the freedom and wholeness God has for you, what would you like to see the Holy Spirit work specifically in your life now?

_____

_____

_____

_____

_____

————————

PRAY THE PRAYER ON PAGES 31-32 IN THE BOOK.

Led to Receive the Inheritance Laid Up for You as God's Child

15. Read Romans 8:13-17. What happens when we live according to the flesh?

_____

_____

_____

_____

What happens if we live according to and are led by the Spirit?

_____

_____

_____

_____

If you are led by the Spirit of God, what does that make you?

_____

_____

_____

You did not receive the spirit of what?

_____

_____

_____

You did receive the Spirit of what?

_____

_____

_____

Because the Holy Spirit is in you, He testifies that you are a son or daughter of God. If you are a child of God, what does that mean you are?

_____

_____

_____

16. Read Galatians 4:6-7. What did God do for you because you became a son or daughter of God by receiving Jesus?

_____

_____

_____

17. Read 1 John 3:1-3. How does God show His love for us?

_____

_____

_____

_____

_____

Because you have this hope of seeing Jesus and becoming like Him, what can you do now to facilitate that?

_____

_____

_____

_____

_____

18. Read Galatians 3:26-29. How have you become a child of God?

_____

_____

_____

_____

If you are in Christ, what are you in God's eyes?

_____

_____

_____

_____

19. Read 1 Peter 1:3-5. We are heirs with Christ because God sees the righteousness of Jesus when we receive Him. We do not earn it. We receive it. God's mercy has given us this hope. What does verse 4 say about the inheritance God has for us?

_____

_____

_____

_____

_____

20. Write out a prayer thanking God that you are an heir with Jesus of all the blessings God has bestowed upon Him. Tell Him what you are most thankful for as His child and what you look forward to as a son or daughter of His.

_____

_____

_____

_____

_____

_____

PRAY THE PRAYER ON PAGE 35 IN THE BOOK.

What the Holy Spirit Has Spoken to Me Through the Study of This Chapter

_____

_____

_____

_____

_____

_____

_____

_____

_____

_____

_____

_____

_____

_____

_____

_____

_____

_____

_____

_____

→ ←

WEEK TWO

Read Chapter 2: "Led to Be Filled"
in LEAD ME, HOLY SPIRIT

1. Read John 7:37-39. In light of what Jesus said, what happens to you when you receive Him?

    _____

    _____

    _____

    _____

    Who was Jesus speaking about when He spoke of rivers of living water?

    _____

    _____

    _____

    _____

    Who would receive the living water?

    _____

    _____

    _____

Why was the Holy Spirit not yet given at this time?

_____

_____

_____

_____

Read John 4:13-14. Water here represents the Holy Spirit. What happens when you drink of the water Jesus gives you?

_____

_____

_____

_____

_____

2. In John 7:37-39, "thirst" means to have a spiritual need. If you don't realize that you have a need to be saved, forgiven, or found, then you don't know you are lost in sins and so you will live in condemnation and bear the consequences of that, which is eternal separation from God. "Living water" refers to the Holy Spirit. These verses clearly say that all who receive Jesus receive the Holy Spirit. At that time the Holy Spirit had not been given because Jesus had not yet been crucified, resurrected, glorified, and ascended into heaven. From the time the Holy Spirit fell upon the people at Pentecost, every true believer in Jesus has had the Holy Spirit dwelling in them.

    If you have received Jesus, you have the Holy Spirit in you. Write out a prayer thanking Him for the living water of His Holy Spirit. If you have not received Jesus, write out a prayer asking Jesus to come into your life and give His Holy Spirit to dwell in you. Tell

Him how much you thirst (have a spiritual need) for His living water (His Holy Spirit).

_____

_____

_____

_____

_____

_____

Led to Be Filled with His Power and Might

3. Read 2 Timothy 3:2-5. Because you have the Holy Spirit in you, you have access to God's power. What do the "lovers of pleasure rather than the lovers of God" have?

_____

_____

_____

_____

Those who want to appear religious but reveal their ungodliness by the way they act are impostors. They profess to be a believer but do not change their sinful behavior. We who welcome the Holy Spirit's work in our lives are to do what with regard to them?

_____

_____

_____

_____

4. The Holy Spirit in you allows the power of God to flow through you. That's how God empowers you to do things you could not do on your own. What are some things that you want God to empower you to do at this time in your life that you know you cannot do on your own? Write out your answer as a prayer to God.

_____

_____

_____

_____

_____

5. Read Zechariah 4:6-7. The angel speaking a word from the Lord to Zerubbabel told him he wasn't going to be able to build the temple by human power, but by the power of the Holy Spirit. The obstacles and problems would be removed by the power of God, and He would enable Zerubbabel to build it. What was the Word of the Lord to the mountain?

_____

_____

_____

_____

What would people shout when the capstone was set in place?

_____

_____

_____

_____

Do you have a mountain in your life that you need the Spirit of God to flatten? What is that and what would you like the Holy Spirit to do? Write out your answer as a prayer.

_____

_____

_____

_____

_____

_____

PRAY THE PRAYER ON PAGE 44 IN THE BOOK.

Led to Be Filled with His Truth and Understanding

6. Read John 14:16-17. Who is the Helper Jesus promised to send? What will He do for you?

_____

_____

_____

_____

Why can't the world receive the Holy Spirit?

_____

_____

_____

Who knows the Holy Spirit and why?

_____

_____

_____

7. Read John 16:13-14. What will the Spirit of truth do for you? Why do you need that?

_____

_____

_____

_____

What will the Holy Spirit do for Jesus?

_____

_____

_____

_____

8. Read Psalm 51:10-11. Before Pentecost, the Holy Spirit would only come *upon* people, but after that He dwells forever *in* all who receive Jesus. Because we have received Jesus, why is David's prayer in verse 11 not applicable for us today?

_____

_____

_____

_____

PRAY THE PRAYER ON PAGES 47-48 IN THE BOOK.

Led to Be Filled with His Wisdom and Revelation

9. Read Ephesians 1:15-17. What did Paul pray for the believers?

    _____

    _____

    _____

    _____

    Read 1 Corinthians 12:3. No one can say Jesus is Lord except by...

    _____

    _____

    _____

    No one can call Jesus accursed if they are...

    _____

    _____

    _____

    Read 1 Corinthians 12:8. How do people receive a word of wisdom?

    _____

    _____

    _____

Read Isaiah 11:2. This Scripture is talking about Jesus. What does it say will rest upon Him?

_____

_____

_____

_____

PRAY THE PRAYER ON PAGES 51-52 IN THE BOOK.

Led to Be Filled with His Love and Hope

10. Read Romans 5:5. How is the love of God poured into our hearts?

_____

_____

_____

_____

If God is love, then His Spirit is love also. Write out a prayer asking the Holy Spirit to fill you with His love for others.

_____

_____

_____

_____

_____

11. Read Romans 15:13. The God of hope also is the Spirit of hope. How do you abound in hope?

_____

_____

_____

Because God's Spirit is in you and your hope is in the Lord, you can overflow with hope. Write out a prayer asking the Lord to help you put your hope in Him by the power of His Spirit in you.

_____

_____

_____

_____

_____

12. Read Galatians 5:5. Where does your hope come from?

_____

_____

_____

_____

What gives _you_ hope? Do you have strong hope in the Lord and His Word? Do you wait hopefully for His return and for your future in heaven? Describe how you feel about that and what you believe with regard to that aspect of your future.

_____

_____

_____

_____

_____

_____

_____

_____

Write out a prayer asking God by His Holy Spirit in you to lead you to consistently put your hope in the Lord no matter what is happening.

_____

_____

_____

_____

_____

_____

_____

PRAY THE PRAYER ON PAGE 55 IN THE BOOK.

WHAT THE HOLY SPIRIT HAS SPOKEN TO ME
THROUGH THE STUDY OF THIS CHAPTER

_____

_____

_____

_____

_____

_____

_____

_____

_____

_____

_____

_____

_____

_____

_____

_____

_____

_____

→ ←

Week Three

Read Chapter 3: "Led to Hear"
in Lead Me, Holy Spirit

1. Read page 58, third paragraph, in the book. Fill in the blanks.

   In order to follow the leading of the Holy Spirit you must _____

   _____

   _____

   _____

   You cannot hear from God reliably if you don't have _____

   _____

   _____

   _____

   _____

Led to Hear God's Word in Your Mind

Read page 59 in the book, fifth paragraph. Fill in the blanks.

You will not be able to hear God speaking to your heart if

_____

_____

_____

_____

Do you ever hear God speaking to your heart when you read His Word? Explain.

_____

_____

_____

_____

2. Read the following Scriptures. Beside each one write what it says about the Word of God.

Colossians 3:16 _____

_____

_____

_____

Hebrews 4:12 _____

_____

_____

_____

2 Timothy 3:16-17 _____

_____

_____

_____

_____

1 Peter 1:24-25 _____

_____

_____

_____

_____

Read the following Scriptures. Beside each one tell what you are to do in response to God's Word and why.

Psalm 119:1-6 _____

_____

_____

_____

_____

James 1:22-25 _____

_____

_____

_____

_____

3. Read Deuteronomy 30:19. Deuteronomy 28:1-14 lists the blessings God promised to pour out on Israel if they would obey Him.
   God was *ready* to bless them and *wanted* to bless them, and He
   said if they diligently obeyed His voice and carefully observed all
   His commandments, He would give them everything they needed.
   Obedience to God's Word puts us in alignment with God's perfect
   will and in a position to receive His blessings.

   In Deuteronomy 28:15-68, God tells the children of Israel of
   the curses that would come upon them if they disobey Him. This
   encompasses everything anyone would not want to happen to them,
   including the unthinkable—which is that they would suffer star-
   vation so terrible that even a previously "sensitive and very refined"
   man or a "tender and delicate" woman would eat their own children (Deuteronomy 28:54-57). They would suffer the worst dis-
   eases with no relief, healing, or recovery (Deuteronomy 28:58-61).
   Those who survive would lose everything and be sold into slavery
   and live in fear. How much worse could it get?

   The Israelites knew God's will for them because He had given
   them specific rules and ways He wanted them to live. They knew
   the consequences for not living His way, and yet they chose to
   do everything He said not to do. God made it clear what His
   response would be if they obeyed Him, and what would happen if they didn't. When things went well for them, they experienced God's blessings. When they forgot the Lord and His laws
   and served other gods, He took away His hand of blessing and
   the curses came to pass.

   The leading of the Holy Spirit will always be to obey God in
   all things. He will never lead us in any other way. We don't want
   to receive God's blessings and then forget His ways and run after
   what we know is not of the Lord and live with the consequences of
   our disobedience. We have a way to avoid all that. God has given
   us His Word and His Holy Spirit *in* us to help us do it.

Write out a prayer asking God to help you understand His Word and remember it. Ask the Holy Spirit to help you do the Word as well.

_____

_____

_____

_____

_____

_____

PRAY THE PRAYER ON PAGES 62-63 IN THE BOOK.

Led to Hear God's Voice to Your Heart

4. Read 1 Corinthians 2:9-10. How does God reveal things to us?

_____

_____

_____

5. Read 1 Corinthians 2:11. How can we know about the things of God?

_____

_____

_____

_____

Read 1 Corinthians 2:12. Because we have the Holy Spirit, what can we know?

_____

_____

_____

_____

Have you ever experienced God revealing something to you by His Holy Spirit? What did He reveal?

_____

_____

_____

_____

How did you respond when God revealed something to you? Did you know it was God right away? Did you ignore it at first? How did you know it was from God?

_____

_____

_____

_____

6. Read John 16:13. What will the Holy Spirit do for you?

_____

_____

_____

Do you feel there have been times when the Holy Spirit has spoken the truth about something to your heart? How did you respond?

_____

_____

_____

_____

_____

PRAY THE PRAYER ON PAGES 67-68 IN THE BOOK.

Led to Hear God's Prompting of Your Spirit

7. Read the top of page 70 in the book. In light of these other words for "prompt," have you ever had a prompting in your mind, soul, or spirit that you believe was God communicating with you through His Holy Spirit? Describe that. If you have never had anything like that, write out a prayer asking God to make you sensitive to His voice and His prompting of your soul and spirit.

_____

_____

_____

_____

8. Read John 14:26. Who will teach you all things, and how will He do it?

_____

_____

_____

_____

Do you ever sense the Holy Spirit in you instructing you? How so? Write out a prayer asking Him to help you always hear His warnings and instructions to your soul.

_____

_____

_____

_____

9. Read Isaiah 30:18-21. These verses talk about the graciousness of God to wait for us to return to Him, and when we do He will hear our fervent prayers. He will bless us when we wait for Him instead of going on our way and trying to make things happen for ourselves. When we go through difficult times, He will help us to see who He has put in our lives to teach us the truth and the right way to walk. And they won't hide the truth. God puts godly pastors and teachers around us from whom we can hear the truth. But our greatest teacher is the Holy Spirit of God in us, who tells us every day which way to walk if we will quiet our mind and soul long enough to listen.

   Do you ever sense the prompting of the Holy Spirit teaching and guiding you as to which way you are to walk? Do you take the time to quiet your soul in order to listen for His prompting? Write out a paragraph to God asking Him to help you hear Him speaking to you by His Holy Spirit as in verse 21.

_____

_____

_____

_____

_____

———•◦•———

PRAY THE PRAYER ON PAGE 71 IN THE BOOK.

Led to Hear God's Will for Your Life

10. Read Ezra 1:1-5. In the book of Ezra, the work of the Holy Spirit is seen as "the hand of the LORD" who moves people to do His will (Ezra 7:6,27-28). In this case God moved the spirits of certain men by the leading of His Spirit to do His will and rebuild His house in Jerusalem. The Holy Spirit in you can move *your* spirit to do His will also. Have you ever been moved by the Holy Spirit to do something you know or strongly feel was God's will? Describe that.

_____

_____

_____

_____

_____

_____

Write out a prayer asking God to stir up your spirit to hear from His Spirit so that you are always led in the perfect will of God.

_____

_____

_____

_____

_____

11. Read Ephesians 1:11-12. What have we been given as believers?

_____

_____

_____

_____

12. Read Ephesians 5:17. What are you supposed to do?

_____

_____

_____

Find out what the will of God is each day and follow the leading of the Holy Spirit. Look in the Word of God and find out what you know is *not* the will of God and don't do that. Find out what the will of God is and do it. Find out what pleases God and do that. According to your Bible, what are some things you know are *always* God's will for you to do?

_____

_____

_____

_____

What are some things you know are *never* God's will for you to do?

_____

_____

_____

_____

Write out a prayer asking God to help you know His will for your
life, especially in any specific area that concerns you right now.

_____

_____

_____

_____

_____

———•••———

PRAY THE PRAYER ON PAGE 74 IN THE BOOK.

WHAT THE HOLY SPIRIT HAS SPOKEN TO ME THROUGH THE STUDY OF THIS CHAPTER

_____

_____

_____

_____

_____

_____

_____

_____

_____

_____

_____

_____

_____

_____

_____

_____

_____

_____

_____

→ ←

WEEK FOUR

Read Chapter 4: "Led to Worship Him"
in LEAD ME, HOLY SPIRIT

Led to Worship Him with Your Whole Heart

1. Read Hebrews 6:4-6. Once you have the Holy Spirit, what should
   you not do and why?

   _____

   _____

   _____

   _____

2. Read Ephesians 4:30. What should you never do with regard to
   the Holy Spirit? How do you think you could do that?

   _____

   _____

   _____

   _____

3. Read the following Scriptures. Beside each one write a brief sum-
   mary of what those verses say about what the condition of your
   heart should be when you communicate with God.

Psalm 111:1 _____

_____

_____

_____

Psalm 119:10 _____

_____

_____

Psalm 119:58 _____

_____

_____

Jeremiah 24:7 _____

_____

_____

Jeremiah 29:12-13 _____

_____

_____

Mark 12:33 _____

_____

_____

_____

4. Read the following Scriptures regarding the Holy Spirit. Write
    out a short prayer of praise after each one using the information
    in those verses as your inspiration.

    Psalm 119:2-3 _____

    _____

    _____

    _____

    John 16:7-8 _____

    _____

    _____

    _____

    Romans 7:6 _____

    _____

    _____

    _____

    Ephesians 3:16 _____

    _____

    _____

    _____

———•◆•———

PRAY THE PRAYER ON PAGE 84 IN THE BOOK.

Led to Worship Him with the Holy Spirit's Help

5. Read Mark 7:6-7. What did Isaiah prophesy about hypocrites? What did that mean about their worship of Him?

    _____

    _____

    _____

    _____

    _____

6. Read 1 Corinthians 2:11-12. Why can the Holy Spirit help you to know how to worship God?

    _____

    _____

    _____

    _____

7. Read Romans 8:26. In light of this Scripture, how can the Holy Spirit help us worship God?

    _____

    _____

    _____

    _____

8. Read Luke 12:11-12. What does Jesus say the Holy Spirit can do for you if you must explain your faith to people in power?

_____

_____

_____

_____

PRAY THE PRAYER ON PAGES 87-88 IN THE BOOK.

Led to Worship Him with Knowledge of the Truth

9. Read Psalm 119:18 and Psalm 119:24. Write out these two Scriptures in your own words as praise to God.

_____

_____

_____

_____

_____

10. Read Psalm 138:2 and Philippians 2:16. What should you praise God for?

_____

_____

_____

_____

11. Read Matthew 24:35. Why can you trust the Word of God?

_____

_____

_____

_____

12. Read John 16:13. Why can the Holy Spirit help you to worship God in truth?

_____

_____

_____

_____

_____

Read John 15:26. What is the Holy Spirit called? Where does He come from?

_____

_____

_____

_____

Read John 4:23. What does God want from true worshippers?

_____

_____

_____

_____

Write out a prayer asking the Holy Spirit to help you be a true worshipper of God.

_____

_____

_____

_____

_____

_____

PRAY THE PRAYER ON PAGES 90-91 IN THE BOOK.

WHAT THE HOLY SPIRIT HAS SPOKEN TO ME THROUGH THE STUDY OF THIS CHAPTER

_____

_____

_____

_____

_____

_____

_____

_____

_____

_____

_____

_____

_____

_____

_____

_____

_____

_____

_____

→ ←

Week Five

Read Chapter 5: "Led to Be Separate"
in Lead Me, Holy Spirit

Led to Be Separate from All Sin

1. Read 1 John 1:8-9. What is true of us if we think we have no sin in us?

_____

_____

_____

_____

_____

How do we get free of sin?

_____

_____

_____

_____

———

PRAY THE PRAYER ON PAGES 97-98 IN THE BOOK.

Led to Be Separate from the World

2. Read Leviticus 20:26. What did God ask of His people? Why?

    _____

    _____

    _____

    Read 2 Corinthians 6:17. What does God ask of us?

    _____

    _____

    _____

3. Read 2 Corinthians 7:1. What does God say to do in order to keep ourselves separated to Him?

    _____

    _____

    _____

    _____

    _____

    _____

    Read 1 John 2:15-17. What are we to do? Why?

    _____

    _____

    _____

Read the following Scriptures. Beside each one write what we are to separate ourselves from.

Deuteronomy 6:14-15 _____

_____

_____

_____

_____

Deuteronomy 7:26 _____

_____

_____

_____

_____

Write out a prayer asking God to show you if there is anything you need to separate yourself from now.

_____

_____

_____

_____

_____

_____

———•◦•———

PRAY THE PRAYER ON PAGES 100-101 IN THE BOOK.

Led to Be Separate from the Enemy

4. Read Ephesians 5:15-16 and 1 Thessalonians 5:22. Write them out as a prayer to God. (For example, "Lord, help me to…")

    _____

    _____

    _____

    _____

    _____

5. Read 1 Peter 5:8 and Psalm 97:10. What are you supposed to do to be separate from the plans of the enemy? What will God do?

    _____

    _____

    _____

    _____

    Write out a prayer asking God to make you wise enough to never fall for any of the enemy's ploys or traps. Ask Him to show you anything specific that you are doing or not doing that gives place to any of the enemy's plans.

    _____

    _____

_____

_____

_____

———•••———

PRAY THE PRAYER ON PAGES 104-105 IN THE BOOK.

Led to Be Separate from All Temptation

6. Read Matthew 26:40-41. What does Jesus say we are to do with regard to temptation? Why?

_____

_____

_____

_____

Read Luke 11:4. Read the fourth paragraph on page 105 in the book. Does this Scripture imply that God will put temptation in your path unless you pray?

_____

_____

_____

What does "Do not lead us into temptation" (Luke 11:4) mean?

_____

_____

_____

Read Hebrews 2:18. How is it that we have an advocate in Jesus with regard to our temptations?

_____

_____

_____

Is temptation a sin? (See page 108 in the book, third paragraph.)

What is the sin with regard to temptation?

_____

_____

_____

PRAY THE PRAYER ON PAGE 109 IN THE BOOK.

Led to Be Separate from the Past

7. Read Isaiah 43:18-19. What are we supposed to do with the past? What will God do when we do that?

_____

_____

_____

_____

_____

8. Read Philippians 3:13-14. What did Paul do with regard to the past?

_____

_____

_____

_____

_____

Write out a prayer to God asking Him to help you do what Paul did.

_____

_____

_____

_____

_____

PRAY THE PRAYER ON PAGE 112 IN THE BOOK.

Led to Be Separate from All Pride

9. Read 2 Chronicles 32:24-26. What happened to Hezekiah because of his pride? What did he do to avoid the wrath of God?

_____

_____

_____

_____

10. Read Proverbs 11:2 and Proverbs 29:23. Write out a prayer inspired by these Scriptures asking God to spare you from the consequences of pride mentioned in them. Ask the Holy Spirit to reveal any pride in you so you can humble yourself and receive the blessings that are mentioned here.

_____

_____

_____

_____

Read Psalm 138:6. How does God relate to humble people? How does He relate to prideful people?

_____

_____

_____

_____

Write out a prayer asking God to keep you from ever giving place to pride in your heart.

_____

_____

_____

_____

_____

PRAY THE PRAYER ON PAGES 115-116 IN THE BOOK.

Led to Be Separate from All That Draws You Away from God

11. Read Judges 2:1-3. The Angel of the Lord is sometimes described as God Himself, and it seems to be so here because He is the one who led the children of Israel out of Egypt and into the Promised Land. He told them to make no covenant with the people in the land and to tear down their altars. They were not to make any compromises whatsoever. But the Israelites did not obey Him. What did God tell them would happen if they did not drive the godless people out?

_____

_____

_____

_____

_____

_____

We have to separate ourselves from anything that comes between us and God and draws us away from obeying Him. Otherwise, it will be a snare to us too. The result of not driving out the ungodly people completely, and not getting rid of their gods as the Lord commanded them to, was that God's anger was against them. The children of Israel forsook God and served Baal instead. So God delivered them into the hands of their enemies (Judges 2:11-14). They had everything going for them, but they did not separate themselves as God had instructed them to do. This is a perfect example of failure through compromise.

Write out a prayer asking God if there is any compromise or snares in your life that separate you from Him in any way. Write down whatever He reveals to you.

_____

_____

_____

_____

_____

_____

_____

12. Read Deuteronomy 29:14-19. What was the covenant and oath being made with the people and what would turn their heart away from God?

_____

_____

_____

_____

_____

_____

PRAY THE PRAYER ON PAGE 119 IN THE BOOK.

What the Holy Spirit Has Spoken to Me Through the Study of This Chapter

_____

_____

_____

_____

_____

_____

_____

_____

_____

_____

_____

_____

_____

_____

_____

_____

_____

_____

_____

_____

→ ←

WEEK SIX

Read Chapter 6: "Led to Be Transformed"
in LEAD ME, HOLY SPIRIT

1. Read 2 Corinthians 3:13-16. What was over the face of Moses and why? (verse 13)

_____

_____

_____

_____

Even today the minds of people are blinded. Why is that? (verses 14-15)

_____

_____

_____

_____

What takes the veil away? (verse 16)

_____

_____

_____

_____

Led to Be Transformed in Your Mind

2. Read 2 Corinthians 3:18. What is true for those of us who have received the Lord?

    _____

    _____

    _____

    _____

    Whose image are you being transformed into when you look to the Lord? How does that happen?

    _____

    _____

    _____

    _____

3. Read Romans 12:2. Do you remember in chapter 5 the section called "Led to Be Separate from the World"? This is the same thing. We are not to allow the world to mold us into its image, but instead we are to get rid of mind-sets and worldviews that do not reflect the ways of God. The world builds its own system so that it can live without God. It is anti-God. What does God want you to do instead?

    _____

    _____

    _____

    _____

    _____

What happens when your mind is renewed?

_____

_____

_____

_____

Write out a prayer asking God to renew your mind every time you read His Word, pray, or worship Him. Ask Him to help you make good choices about what you allow into your mind every day.

_____

_____

_____

_____

4. Read Ephesians 4:17-24. In what manner are you to never walk once you receive Jesus? (verses 17-19)

_____

_____

_____

_____

How does God want you to walk? (verses 20-24)

_____

_____

_____

_____

Write out a prayer inspired by Ephesians 4:17-24 asking God to help you walk the right way every day.

_____

_____

_____

_____

_____

Read Romans 8:5-6. What does God want you to do with your mind?

_____

_____

_____

_____

What does God *not* want you to do with your mind?

_____

_____

_____

_____

5. Read the following Scriptures and beside each one write what you are to do or *not* to do with your mind.

Matthew 22:37_____

_____

_____

_____

Ephesians 4:17 _____

_____

_____

_____

2 Corinthians 10:5 _____

_____

_____

_____

2 Corinthians 11:3 _____

_____

_____

_____

2 Timothy 1:7 _____

_____

_____

_____

PRAY THE PRAYER ON PAGES 126-127 IN THE BOOK.

Led to Be Transformed in Your Emotions

6. Read 2 Corinthians 3:17. God wants you liberated from everything that keeps you from becoming all He made you to be. Where
   do you find that kind of freedom?

_____

_____

_____

_____

Write out a prayer thanking Jesus that He set you free from sin, death, condemnation, and everything that separates you from God and keeps you from moving into all He has for you.

_____

_____

_____

_____

7. Read Proverbs 4:20-23. What are you to do with God's Word and why?

_____

_____

_____

_____

What are you to do with regard to your heart?

_____

_____

_____

_____

_____

Write out a prayer asking God to help you keep control of your heart.

_____

_____

_____

_____

_____

8.   Read Psalm 34:18 and Proverbs 15:13. What do these Scriptures say about having a broken heart?

_____

_____

_____

_____

Have you ever had a broken heart? Do you feel you are still suffering from that in some way now? Write out your answer as a prayer asking God to heal your damaged or broken heart. If you have never had a broken heart or you have already been healed from that, write out a prayer of thanksgiving to God for it.

_____

_____

_____

_____

_____

9. Read Philippians 4:6-7. What are you to do with any anxieties you have?

_____

_____

_____

_____

_____

_____

What will happen when you pray? What will guard your heart?

_____

_____

_____

_____

_____

———————

PRAY THE PRAYER ON PAGES 129-130 IN THE BOOK.

Led to Be Transformed in Your Character

10. The Holy Spirit in us can transform who we *are* into all we were *created to be*. He always wants to change us for the better because His goal is to lead us to become more like the Lord. None of us has attained that yet, so we will always need to be changed. In what ways would you like the Holy Spirit to transform your character?

Write out your answer as a prayer to God. If you need to review what character is, read the first two paragraphs under the "Led to Be Transformed" section title on pages 130-131 in the book.

_____

_____

_____

_____

_____

11. Read Romans 5:1-5. Fill in the blanks.

We are justified by _____, we have peace with God

through _____,

and we can glory in tribulation because it produces _____

_____,

which produces _____,

which produces _____

Why are we never disappointed by putting our hope in God?

_____

_____

_____

12. Read Titus 3:3-7. How did we behave before we received Jesus? (verse 3)

_____

_____

_____

_____

What happened after we received Jesus? (verses 4-6)

_____

_____

_____

_____

_____

Now that we are justified by God's grace, what have we become? (verse 7)

_____

_____

_____

_____

_____

PRAY THE PRAYER ON PAGES 132-133 IN THE BOOK.

What the Holy Spirit Has Spoken to Me Through the Study of This Chapter

_____

_____

_____

_____

_____

_____

_____

_____

_____

_____

_____

_____

_____

_____

_____

_____

_____

_____

➤ ◄

Week Seven

Read Chapter 7: "Led to See Purpose"
in Lead Me, Holy Spirit

Led to See Purpose in Your Reason for Getting Up Every Day

1. Read Lamentations 3:22-24. What are your reasons for getting up every morning? What motivates you to keep going in difficult times?

_____

_____

_____

_____

2. Read Psalm 96:2. What is another good reason to get up in the morning? Do you feel hope in your heart because you serve God each day?

_____

_____

_____

_____

3. Read Hebrews 12:28. How are we to serve God?

_____

_____

_____

What does God give us to help us serve Him well?

_____

_____

_____

———•••———

PRAY THE PRAYER ON PAGES 138-139 IN THE BOOK.

Led to See Purpose in the Gifts God Has Put in You

4. Read James 1:16-17. Where does every good and perfect gift come from?

_____

_____

_____

_____

If all good gifts come from God, how do you think you should use your gifts?

_____

_____

_____

Write out a prayer asking the Holy Spirit to lead you in the use of your gifts according to God's will.

_____

_____

_____

_____

5. Read Ephesians 4:7. What has Jesus given to you because you have received Him as your Lord? Write out your answer as a prayer of thanks to Him for that.

_____

_____

_____

_____

6. What are some of the gifts God has put in you that you can use to serve Him and help others according to His will? If you don't know or are not sure, write out a prayer asking God to reveal them to you. Write down anything you feel God speaking to your heart about that.

_____

_____

_____

_____

7. Read Romans 11:29. God does not ever take back the gifts He has put in you. His call on your life will always be there. His purpose

for your life never changes. What comfort does this Scripture give with regard to the gifts and calling God has for your life?

_____

_____

_____

_____

—•⋅◦⋅•—

PRAY THE PRAYER ON PAGES 144-145 IN THE BOOK.

Led to See Purpose in God's Call on Your Life

8. Read Ephesians 1:15-19. We need the spirit of wisdom and revelation and knowledge of the Lord in order to know what?

_____

_____

_____

_____

9. Read 2 Timothy 1:8-9. Not only has God delivered us from the consequences of our sin because of the sacrifice of His Son Jesus, but He has also done what for us?

_____

_____

_____

_____

10. Read 2 Thessalonians 1:11. Write out a prayer asking God to help you to walk worthy of His call on your life so you can fulfill your purpose.

_____

_____

_____

_____

11. Read 1 Corinthians 1:26-29. Do you ever feel you are not qualified to move into your calling? What do these Scriptures say about that? Who has God called and why?

_____

_____

_____

_____

_____

12. Read Ephesians 4:1. Your walk is the way you live your life. God has called you for a purpose. Don't walk as if you are not called by God and have no purpose. In light of this verse, how are you supposed to walk? How can you do that?

_____

_____

_____

_____

PRAY THE PRAYER ON PAGES 149-150 IN THE BOOK.

What the Holy Spirit Has Spoken to Me Through the Study of This Chapter

> ⇥ ⇤

WEEK EIGHT

Read Chapter 8: "Led to Bear Good Fruit"
in LEAD ME, HOLY SPIRIT

1. Read Matthew 7:15-20. How can you identify a false prophet?

    _____

    _____

    _____

    What will a good tree produce?

    _____

    _____

    _____

    What is a good tree *unable* to produce?

    _____

    _____

    _____

    What happens to a bad tree that does not bear good fruit?

    _____

    _____

    _____

Read Matthew 13:22-23. Who bears good fruit?

_____

_____

_____

_____

2. Read Galatians 5:22-23. What are the nine fruits that the Holy Spirit produces in us? Write down each one, and under it write whether you feel you need more of that fruit in your life and why you think that. Write out your answer as a prayer. (For example, "Holy Spirit, fill me with more of Your patience, because I run short on that way too often.")

The first fruit of the Spirit is _____

_____

_____

_____

The second fruit of the Spirit is _____

_____

_____

_____

The third fruit of the Spirit is _____

_____

_____

_____

The fourth fruit of the Spirit is _____

_____

_____

_____

The fifth fruit of the Spirit is _____

_____

_____

_____

The sixth fruit of the Spirit is _____

_____

_____

_____

The seventh fruit of the Spirit is _____

_____

_____

_____

The eighth fruit of the Spirit is _____

_____

_____

_____

The ninth fruit of the Spirit is _____

_____

_____

_____

Led to Bear Good Fruit in Your Life

3. Read Mark 4:30-32. What did Jesus compare the kingdom of God to and how so?

    _____

    _____

    _____

    _____

    Have you ever planted a small seed into your life and watched it grow into something big? Describe that.

    _____

    _____

    _____

    _____

    Write out a prayer asking the Holy Spirit to multiply the seed of God's Word in you each time you read it so that it grows into something great.

    _____

    _____

    _____

    _____

4. Read John 15:5-8. In these verses, who is Jesus?

_____

_____

_____

_____

In these verses, who are you?

_____

_____

_____

_____

What happens if you do not abide in Jesus?

_____

_____

_____

_____

What happens if you abide in Jesus and His words abide in you?

_____

_____

_____

_____

How much can you do without Jesus in your life?

_____

_____

_____

_____

Write out a prayer asking God to help you live your life in Him and His Word using those Scriptures as your inspiration. Don't forget to include verse 8.

_____

_____

_____

_____

_____

5. Read John 15:1-4. Who is Jesus?

_____

_____

_____

Who is God?

_____

_____

_____

Why do you need to abide in Jesus?

_____

_____

What does God do with the branches that do not bear fruit?

What does God do with the branches that bear fruit?

When we are being pruned, God gets rid of everything that is not necessary in our lives in order to produce more fruit in the future. Have you ever felt as though God is pruning you? How did that make you feel? What was the result of that season? If you have never had that experience, or are not sure if you have, write out a prayer asking God to help you recognize His pruning process so that you can cooperate with Him and not resist what He is doing in your life.

Is there something God has stripped away from your life in the past, or that you know God is wanting to be gone from your life now?

_____

_____

_____

_____

_____

_____

6. Read Ephesians 5:8-11. How are you to walk and why?

_____

_____

_____

The fruit of the Spirit manifests itself as what? (verse 9)

_____

_____

_____

How are you to respond to the unfruitful works of darkness? (verse 11)

_____

_____

_____

PRAY THE PRAYER ON PAGES 156-157 IN THE BOOK.

Led to Bear Good Fruit in Your Work

7. Read Colossians 1:9-10. In your own words, what did Paul constantly pray for the people he was writing to?

_____

_____

_____

_____

_____

Write out a similar prayer specific to your own life.

_____

_____

_____

_____

_____

Write out a prayer for one or two other people, specifically using their names and these verses as your inspiration and model.

_____

_____

_____

_____

8. Read Proverbs 22:29. The work you do will always have a lot to do with the doors of opportunity God opens for you. He may open the door to different jobs, different ministries, or different roles (such as parenting, etc.), and He wants you to bear fruit in all of them. Whatever you are doing now as work, write out a prayer asking God to bless it and make it fruitful and open doors no man can close so you can bear even more fruit.

_____

_____

_____

_____

_____

_____

If you are not certain that you are where you are supposed to be right now, write out a prayer asking the Holy Spirit to lead you to the right work in order to fulfill what He has for you to accomplish or learn. If you are in the right work, write out a prayer thanking Him for that and asking Him to always open the door of opportunities He wants you to go through.

_____

_____

_____

_____

_____

_____

9. Read Psalm 92:12-15. What is true of the righteous—those who
   know Jesus?

   _____

   _____

   _____

   _____

   _____

   What is true of *your* future because you know Jesus?

   _____

   _____

   _____

   _____

   _____

   Write out a prayer thanking God that because you know Jesus
   and have the Holy Spirit in you, you will be fruitful all of your
   life. Ask Him to help you to be an effective minister of the fruit
   of His Holy Spirit to others until you go to be with Him.

   _____

   _____

   _____

   _____

   _____

   _____

PRAY THE PRAYER ON PAGES 160-161 IN THE BOOK.

Led to Bear Good Fruit in Your Relationships

10. Read Ecclesiastes 4:9-10. What is the advantage of good and fruitful relationships?

_____

_____

_____

_____

_____

Read Amos 3:3. What is a big obstacle to successful relationships?

_____

_____

_____

_____

11. Read the following Scriptures. Write next to them what you must have to enjoy fruitful relationships. Write your answer as a prayer. (For example, "Lord, help me to be…")

Proverbs 18:24 _____

_____

_____

_____

Proverbs 24:21-22 _____

_____

_____

_____

_____

Proverbs 27:9_____

_____

_____

_____

_____

Proverbs 17:17_____

_____

_____

_____

_____

2 Corinthians 6:14-15_____

_____

_____

_____

_____

Proverbs 24:21-22 _____

_____

_____

_____

12. Read Galatians 5:25-26. If we are walking in the Spirit, what will we not do in our relationships?

_____

_____

_____

_____

Read 1 John 1:7. What happens because we walk in the light— or in the Spirit?

_____

_____

_____

_____

Read John 13:34-35. What is the new commandment Jesus gave, and how should that affect your relationships and make them fruitful?

_____

_____

_____

_____

_____

_____

Do you feel you have an abundance of love in your relationships? Write out your answer as a prayer explaining what you would like to see happen in the relationships that most concern you or are most valuable to you. If you feel you have a lack of good, solid, and fruitful relationships, write that out in your prayer and tell God the longing of your heart in that regard.

_____

_____

_____

_____

_____

_____

_____

_____

PRAY THE PRAYER ON PAGE 163 IN THE BOOK.

What the Holy Spirit Has Spoken to Me Through the Study of This Chapter

_____

_____

_____

_____

_____

_____

_____

_____

_____

_____

_____

_____

_____

_____

_____

_____

_____

_____

_____

→ ←

Week Nine

Read Chapter 9: "Led to Discern"
in Lead Me, Holy Spirit

1. Read Hebrews 5:12-14. In these verses, Paul is talking to people who had been taught about the Lord and His ways for so long that they should have been teaching others by that time, but instead they still needed to be taught. Just like a child who never eats solid food and only drinks milk, affecting his growth, there is growth or lack of it in our spirit as well. That happens when we *hear* the Word and do not *do* the Word, and as a result we lose our spiritual discernment. What is true of those who only drink milk?

    _____

    _____

    _____

    Who does the solid food belong to?

    _____

    _____

    _____

    We must desire discernment and be aware of how much we need it. Write out a prayer asking God to help you grow in His Word and have the discernment He wants you to have.

    _____

    _____

_____

_____

_____

_____

2. Read Ephesians 4:14. Other words for discernment are "perception" and "insight." Discernment is the ability to see accurately. In light of this Scripture, why do we need to grow up spiritually and gain spiritual discernment, perception, and insight?

_____

_____

_____

_____

_____

Led to Discern God Guiding You

3. Read 1 Corinthians 2:14. Complete the following sentence.

The natural man does not receive _____

_____

_____

Why can't the natural man know the things of the Spirit?

_____

_____

_____

4. Read 1 Corinthians 3:1-3. Why were the Corinthians unable to receive solid food instead of milk?

    _____

    _____

    _____

    What are some signs of being carnal?

    _____

    _____

    _____

5. Read John 16:12-14. Who is your guide?

    _____

    _____

    _____

    What does the Holy Spirit do?

    _____

    _____

    _____

    _____

    _____

    Read 2 Corinthians 3:1-3. Paul had taught the Christians at Corinth and they had become like a letter from Jesus. Where was this epistle written and who wrote it?

    _____

_____

_____

_____

6. Read Ruth 3:1. The story of Ruth in the Bible does not mention the Holy Spirit, but Naomi—Ruth's mother-in-law, whose late son was Ruth's husband—typifies the Holy Spirit in the way she guided Ruth in securing her future. Just as the Holy Spirit directs our path when we seek Him for His leading and follow His promptings, Naomi had Ruth's best interests at heart when she advised her. And Ruth lovingly served Naomi and *received her counsel* instead of going her own way.

Ruth could have said, "All I want is to have some fun, and my mother-in-law is trying to tell me what to do. I'm out of here to find my own way." But she didn't because she knew God was guiding her to stay with Naomi.

Because of Naomi's guidance and Ruth's humble submission to her leading, God opened the way for Ruth to find her future husband. It is a wonderful example of how God redeems our difficult situations, and not only uses them for His purpose and glory, but also for *our* greatest blessing. But we have to be led by His Spirit and be able to hear His direction through another godly person when necessary.

Have you ever discerned the Holy Spirit guiding you to do something and you knew it was God? Explain. If not, write out a paragraph asking God to help you have insight when He is guiding you to do something.

_____

_____

_____

_____

_____

_____

Have you ever recognized the Lord leading you through someone else's advice? Describe that. If you have never experienced that,
write out a prayer asking God to give you the discernment to recognize when that is happening. Ask Him to also enable you to
discern when someone's advice is *not* from God.

_____

_____

_____

_____

_____

———•···•———

PRAY THE PRAYER ON PAGES 172-173 IN THE BOOK.

Led to Discern God Blessing You

7. Read Proverbs 10:22. What is one way you can discern whether
    the blessing in your life is from God? Keep in mind that "rich"
    doesn't necessarily mean money, although it can. It means a life
    rich in the things of God. It means family, good health, solid rela-
    tionships, and having a life that works and glorifies God.

_____

_____

_____

_____

_____

_____

8. Read the following Scriptures. Beside each one describe who is blessed and how they are blessed, if it states that. Not all are specific about what the blessing is, but any blessing from God is good. If *you* fall into any of these categories what can you expect as a blessing from God?

Luke 12:37 _____

_____

_____

_____

John 20:29 _____

_____

_____

_____

Acts 20:35 _____

_____

_____

_____

Romans 4:7 _____

_____

_____

_____

James 1:12_____

_____

_____

_____

James 1:25_____

_____

_____

_____

9. Read Matthew 5:3-12. Fill in the blanks and answer the question.

Blessed are (verse 3) _____

for theirs is _____

What blessing can you expect to receive from God? When? (For example, "When I am feeling sad, empty, or discouraged, God will...") _____

_____

_____

_____

_____

_____

Blessed are (verse 4) _____

for they shall _____

What can you expect that God will do for you? When? _____

_____

_____

_____

_____

_____

Blessed are (verse 5) _____

for they shall _____

What can you expect to receive from God? When? _____

_____

_____

_____

_____

_____

Blessed are (verse 6) _____

for they shall _____

What can you expect to receive from God? When? _____

_____

_____

_____

_____

_____

Blessed are (verse 7) _____

for they shall _____

What can you expect from God? When? _____

_____

_____

_____

_____

_____

Blessed are (verse 8) _____

for they shall _____

What can you expect from God? When? _____

_____

_____

_____

_____

_____

Blessed are (verse 9) _____

for they shall _____

What can you expect from God? When? _____

_____

_____

_____

_____

Blessed are (verse 10) _____

for theirs is _____

What can you expect God will do when you are persecuted for your faith in Him? _____

_____

_____

_____

_____

_____

Blessed are (verses 11-12) _____

_____

_____

_____

Rejoice and be exceedingly glad for _____

_____

_____

_____

PRAY THE PRAYER ON PAGE 177 IN THE BOOK.

Led to Discern God Protecting You

10. Read the following Scriptures. Beside each one describe what kind of protection God gives us.

Psalm 121:3-8 _____

_____

_____

_____

_____

Psalm 124:1-5_____

_____

_____

_____

_____

Isaiah 41:10 _____

_____

_____

_____

_____

John 10:28-30 _____

_____

_____

_____

_____

_____

11. Read the following Scriptures. Beside each one describe what God protects us from in our lives.

Psalm 56:9_____

_____

_____

_____

Psalm 57:1_____

_____

_____

_____

Psalm 91:3-7_____

_____

_____

_____

1 Corinthians 10:13_____

_____

_____

_____

Jude 24 _____

_____

_____

_____

12. Read the following Scriptures. Beside each one write what God has said He will do.

Psalm 23:4_____

_____

_____

_____

Psalm 37:17_____

_____

_____

_____

Psalm 145:20_____

_____

_____

_____

Proverbs 3:26_____

_____

_____

_____

Proverbs 14:26_____

_____

_____

_____

2 Thessalonians 3:3_____

_____

_____

_____

In light of the Scriptures in questions 10-12, has God been protecting you in ways you haven't thought about? Do you believe God has protected you in ways you don't even realize? Write out a prayer of thanksgiving for how God has protected you in the past. Ask Him to help you discern the ways He protects you so that you will thank Him and not resist Him.

_____

_____

_____

_____

_____

_____

PRAY THE PRAYER ON PAGE 180 IN THE BOOK.

What the Holy Spirit Has Spoken to Me Through the Study of This Chapter

_____

_____

_____

_____

_____

_____

_____

_____

_____

_____

_____

_____

_____

_____

_____

_____

_____

_____

_____

_____

Week Ten

Read Chapter 10: "Led to Pray"
in LEAD ME, HOLY SPIRIT

1. Read Romans 8:26 again. (You looked it up in Week 4, but it is important to refresh your memory here.) What does the Holy Spirit do for you and why?

_____

_____

_____

_____

_____

Do you ever have times when you don't know what to pray? Write out a prayer asking God to give you words to pray whenever you need them by the power of His Spirit in you.

_____

_____

_____

_____

_____

2. Read Ephesians 3:14-19. In your own words, what did Paul pray for the Ephesians? Write it as a prayer for yourself or someone else.

_____

_____

_____

_____

_____

3. Read Matthew 21:22 and John 14:13-14. What does Jesus say about prayer?

_____

_____

_____

_____

_____

Read Matthew 7:7. What are we to *keep* on doing? What will happen?

_____

_____

_____

_____

Led to Pray for the Burdens on Your Heart

4. Read Philippians 4:6-7. What should you do with the things that weigh heavily on your heart?

_____

_____

_____

_____

_____

Write down the most pressing burdens you have in your life right now as a prayer to God.

_____

_____

_____

_____

Read Psalm 138:8. What will God do for you when you have concerns?_____

_____

Write out a prayer telling God your greatest concerns.

_____

_____

_____

_____

Whatever you are going through, take comfort in the fact that when you follow the Lord and bring your concerns before Him, He will work powerfully to bring them to a right conclusion. He will take the things that concern you and work them out.

———

PRAY THE PRAYER ON PAGES 186-187 IN THE BOOK.

Led to Pray for Your Land

5.   Read 2 Chronicles 7:14. What are we supposed to do with regard to the land we live in?

_____

_____

_____

_____

_____

What are the things that most concern you about the city and county you live in? Ask the Holy Spirit to lead you as you write down whatever He brings to your mind to pray about.

_____

_____

_____

_____

_____

PRAY THE PRAYER ON PAGE 189 IN THE BOOK.

Led to Pray for Others

6.   Read Galatians 6:2 and Ephesians 6:18. What are you to do with regard to others?

_____

_____

_____

_____

_____

Who are the people most on your mind to pray for at this time? Ask the Holy Spirit to tell you who He wants you to pray for and write their name below as He brings them to mind. Then pray for each one as the Spirit leads you.

_____

_____

_____

_____

PRAY THE PRAYER ON PAGE 193 IN THE BOOK.

Led to Pray for Miracles

7. Read Mark 9:23-24. What did Jesus say as He was about to do a miracle?

    _____

    _____

    _____

    What did the father say back to Him? Write out your answer as your own prayer to the Lord for this same thing.

    _____

    _____

_____

_____

Read John 14:12-13. What did Jesus say?

_____

_____

_____

_____

Do you believe what Jesus said? Why or why not?

_____

_____

_____

_____

8. Read Mark 6:5-6. Why did Jesus not do many works there in His own community?

_____

_____

_____

_____

Write out a prayer asking God to give you the faith you need to believe for any miracle He wants to do in your life. Ask Him to take away all doubt in His ability and desire to work a miracle for you.

_____

_____

_____

_____

_____

_____

—◦◦◦◦◦—

PRAY THE PRAYER ON PAGE 196 IN THE BOOK.

Led to Pray for Healing

9. Read the following Scriptures. What do they say with regard to the healing power of Jesus?

    Psalm 103:2-3_____

    _____

    _____

    Psalm 107:20_____

    _____

    _____

    Isaiah 53:5_____

    _____

    _____

    Jeremiah 30:17_____

    _____

    _____

Malachi 4:2 _____

_____

_____

Matthew 8:17_____

_____

_____

1 Peter 2:22-24 _____

_____

_____

10. Read the following Scriptures. Next to each one, write down what we must do in order to receive healing.

Isaiah 58:6,8_____

_____

_____

James 5:14-15_____

_____

_____

James 5:16 _____

_____

_____

_____

Choose two or more of the Scriptures above and write them out
as a prayer to God for your own healing or the healing of someone you care about.

_____

_____

_____

_____

——◦·•·◦——

PRAY THE PRAYER ON PAGE 200 IN THE BOOK.

Led to Pray for as Long as It Takes

11. Read the following Scriptures. Beside each one describe what you
    are to stand fast in.

    1 Corinthians 16:13_____

    _____

    _____

    Galatians 5:1_____

    _____

    _____

    1 Thessalonians 3:8_____

    _____

    _____

12. Read Luke 18:1. What do you need to always do without fail?

_____

_____

_____

_____

Read Ephesians 6:13-14. How are you to keep standing when everything is falling apart?

_____

_____

_____

_____

Write out a prayer asking God to help you keep standing strong no matter what is happening in your life or around you.

_____

_____

_____

_____

PRAY THE PRAYER ON PAGE 203 IN THE BOOK.

What the Holy Spirit Has Spoken to Me Through the Study of This Chapter

Week Eleven

Read Chapter 11: "Led to Follow God"
in Lead Me, Holy Spirit

Led to Follow God to an Intimate Day-by-Day Walk with Him

1. Read 2 Chronicles 15:1-4. What is the way to make sure that the Lord is walking with you? (verse 2)

    _____

    _____

    _____

    _____

    When Israel was living without God, what happened?

    _____

    _____

    _____

2. Read Galatians 3:2-3. Do you have a tendency to take control of your life and make things happen as opposed to walking with the leading of the Holy Spirit? Explain. What do these verses say about that?

_____

_____

_____

_____

Read Colossians 2:6-7. How are you supposed to walk with God?

_____

_____

_____

_____

God wants you to live a life you cannot live without Him. That means you have to be dependent on Him for every step you take. That means you have to live led by the Holy Spirit—a day-by-day, step-by-step walk with God. Write out a prayer asking God for that kind of intimate walk with Him.

_____

_____

_____

_____

PRAY THE PRAYER ON PAGES 208-209 IN THE BOOK.

Led to Follow God to Purify the Words You Speak

3. Read the following Scriptures. Write next to them what God requires of you with regard to the words you speak.

Proverbs 18:21 _____

_____

_____

_____

Ephesians 4:29 _____

_____

_____

_____

Philippians 2:14 _____

_____

_____

_____

2 Timothy 2:16 _____

_____

_____

_____

1 Peter 3:10 _____

_____

_____

_____

4.   Read Luke 6:45. Where do the words we speak come from?

_____

_____

_____

_____

How, then, can you purify the words you speak?

_____

_____

_____

_____

———•◦•———

PRAY THE PRAYER ON PAGES 211-212 IN THE BOOK.

Led to Follow God to Mountain-Moving Steps of Faith

5. Read Romans 12:3. Where do we initially find faith?

_____

_____

_____

_____

Read Romans 10:17. How do we increase our faith?

_____

_____

_____

_____

Read Mark 11:22-24. How should we pray?

_____

_____

_____

_____

6. Read the following Scriptures. Beside each one write what your faith in the Lord can do or has done for you.

Galatians 2:20_____

_____

_____

Romans 5:1_____

_____

_____

Read James 1:6-8. How are we to pray?

_____

_____

_____

What happens if we don't pray in faith?

_____

_____

_____

Read Romans 14:23. What happens if we live without faith?

_____

_____

_____

Write out a prayer asking God to increase your faith until it moves mountains in your life.

_____

_____

_____

_____

———❖———

PRAY THE PRAYER ON PAGE 215 IN THE BOOK.

Led to Follow God to the Company of Godly People

7. Read 2 Corinthians 6:14-16. With what kind of people are you to establish your most important relationships?

_____

_____

_____

Read Proverbs 12:26. What happens if you have relationships with ungodly people?

_____

_____

_____

_____

8. Read the following Scriptures. Next to each one tell how we are to
   establish our relationships.

   Matthew 5:23-24_____

   _____

   _____

   Luke 17:3-4_____

   _____

   _____

   John 13:34-35_____

   _____

   _____

   Hebrews 10:24-25_____

   _____

   _____

   1 John 1:7_____

   _____

   _____

If you have a relationship with anyone who is not a believer, write out a prayer asking God to lead that person to Jesus so they can be born into His kingdom.

_____

_____

_____

_____

_____

—◆•◆•◆—

PRAY THE PRAYER ON PAGES 217-218 IN THE BOOK.

Led to Follow God to Care for Your Body

9.   Read 1 Corinthians 3:16-17. What should you always remember about your body?

_____

_____

_____

What happens if you defile your body in any way? Why?

_____

_____

_____

_____

Read Romans 12:1. What are you supposed to do with your body?

_____

_____

_____

_____

Do you have trouble caring for your body properly? Don't feel badly if you do because you are not alone. Nearly everyone struggles with some aspect of proper body care. Write out a prayer asking God to help you care for your body the way you should. Ask the Holy Spirit to teach you and guide you and give you an abundance of the fruit of the Spirit called self-control. Ask Him to help you care for His dwelling place in you.

_____

_____

_____

_____

PRAY THE PRAYER ON PAGES 220-221 IN THE BOOK.

Led to Follow God to Resist the Enemy's Attacks

10. Read Luke 10:17-20. What did Jesus say to His 70 disciples?

_____

_____

_____

_____

Over what did Jesus give them authority?

_____

_____

_____

What were they to rejoice over most of all?

_____

_____

_____

11. Read Isaiah 59:19. What will the Holy Spirit do for you when the enemy attacks you?

_____

_____

_____

Write out a prayer of thanksgiving to the Lord that He has defeated the enemy of your soul and that He will protect you from him when you stay close to God and walk with the leading of the Spirit.

_____

_____

_____

_____

_____

_____

——◦•◦——

PRAY THE PRAYER ON PAGE 224 IN THE BOOK.

Led to Follow God to the Right Place at the Right Time

12. Read Judges 6:36-40. Gideon wanted to know he had heard from God, so he put a fleece of wool on the threshing floor. He said that if there was dew on the fleece and not on the ground, then he would know that God was going to use him to save Israel. And that is exactly what happened. But then Gideon wanted another test just to be sure. This time he said, "Let it now be dry only on the fleece, but on all the ground let there be dew." Again, this is exactly what happened.

We should be more like Gideon and refuse to act on impulse. Instead, we should pray first, seek the leading of the Lord, and invite the Holy Spirit to give us direction. Write out a prayer asking the Holy Spirit to help you hear Him leading you. Thank Him that He will always lead you to the right place at the right time.

_____

_____

_____

_____

_____

_____

PRAY THE PRAYER ON PAGE 228 IN THE BOOK.

What the Holy Spirit Has Spoken to Me Through the Study of This Chapter

_____

_____

_____

_____

_____

_____

_____

_____

_____

_____

_____

_____

_____

_____

_____

_____

_____

_____

→ ←

WEEK TWELVE

Read Chapter 12: "Led to Lead"
in LEAD ME, HOLY SPIRIT

1. Read 1 Corinthians 2:4. How did Paul move in his ministry to others? What did he *not* do?

    _____

    _____

    _____

    _____

    When you tell other people about the Lord, don't rely on your own wisdom and words. What should you do instead?

    _____

    _____

    _____

    _____

2. Read Matthew 5:13-16. We are not to just keep getting taught and then keep that information all to ourselves. We are to share what we know with others. How does Jesus want you to view yourself when you minister to others?

    _____

    _____

_____

_____

Read Colossians 4:6 and Mark 9:50. In your own words, what do these Scriptures say about the way you should relate to others?

_____

_____

_____

_____

3. Read Matthew 9:36-38. What was Jesus' concern?

_____

_____

_____

What does Jesus want us to do?

_____

_____

_____

_____

Write out a prayer asking God to help you be a part of doing just that.

_____

_____

_____

_____

4. Read Mark 8:34-38. What does Jesus want His people to do?

_____

_____

_____

_____

What happens if we are reluctant to tell anyone else about the Lord?

_____

_____

_____

_____

Do you ever feel hesitant to share what you know of Jesus? Does it embarrass you to do that? Write your answer out as a prayer to God, asking Him to open doors of opportunity that you know you are to walk through as you are led by the Holy Spirit to communicate the love of Jesus to them.

_____

_____

_____

_____

Led to Lead Others to Find Hope in the Lord

5. Read Romans 5:5. Why will people never be disappointed if they put their hope in God?

_____

_____

_____

_____

6. Read the following Scriptures. Beside each one tell what it means with regard to the hope in your life.

Psalm 33:18_____

_____

_____

Psalm 39:7_____

_____

_____

Romans 15:4 _____

_____

_____

Galatians 5:5_____

_____

_____

2 Thessalonians 2:16 _____

_____

_____

1 Peter 1:3 _____

_____

_____

Write out a prayer asking God to help you point people to the
hope talked about in these Scriptures.

_____

_____

_____

_____

_____

———————

PRAY THE PRAYER ON PAGE 234 IN THE BOOK.

Led to Lead Others to Know the Truth

7. Read John 16:13. Part of leading people to Jesus is to help them
   find God's ultimate truth. The Spirit of truth will lead you in that.
   One of the best ways to impress people with the goodness of God
   is to be a person who lives by God's truth. And to be a person who
   always tells the truth. It's all too rare in this world, and it counts for
   a lot with people who are being drawn to Jesus. Write out a prayer
   with this Scripture as inspiration, asking God to make you a person of the truth and that the Spirit of truth in you will draw people to Him.

   _____

   _____

   _____

   _____

8. Read the following Scriptures. Next to each one write down what it says about truth.

1 Samuel 12:24 _____

_____

_____

John 14:6_____

_____

_____

Ephesians 4:25_____

_____

_____

PRAY THE PRAYER ON PAGES 236-237 IN THE BOOK.

Led to Lead Others to Pray in Power

9. Read the following Scriptures. Beside each one write what we should do for others.

Romans 12:10_____

_____

_____

Romans 15:7_____

_____

_____

_____

1 Corinthians 12:25_____

_____

_____

Galatians 5:13 _____

_____

_____

Ephesians 4:32_____

_____

_____

Ephesians 5:21_____

_____

_____

Hebrews 10:24 _____

_____

_____

1 Thessalonians 5:11_____

_____

_____

10. Read the following Scriptures. What are we to pray for and why?

Matthew 18:19 _____

_____

_____

2 Corinthians 1:3-4 _____

_____

_____

Galatians 6:2 _____

_____

_____

Philippians 2:1-4 _____

_____

_____

James 5:16 _____

_____

_____

1 Timothy 2:1 _____

_____

_____

_____

———◆———

PRAY THE PRAYER ON PAGES 239-240 IN THE BOOK.

Led to Lead Others to Fulfill Their Purpose

11. Read the following Scriptures. Write out what you could tell someone about the purpose God has for him or her.

Romans 8:28 _____

_____

_____

_____

Ephesians 1:11 _____

_____

_____

_____

12. Read the following Scriptures. In light of these verses, what could you tell someone about what God has called them to do?

1 Corinthians 1:9 _____

_____

_____

1 Thessalonians 2:10-12 _____

_____

_____

1 Thessalonians 4:7_____

_____

_____

1 Timothy 6:12_____

_____

_____

2 Timothy 1:8-9_____

_____

_____

2 Peter 1:10-11_____

_____

_____

PRAY THE PRAYER ON PAGES 241-242 IN THE BOOK.

WHAT THE HOLY SPIRIT HAS SPOKEN TO ME THROUGH THE STUDY OF THIS CHAPTER

_____

_____

_____

_____

_____

_____

_____

_____

_____

_____

_____

_____

_____

_____

_____

_____

_____

_____

BOOK OF PRAYERS

STORMIE OMARTIAN

LEAD ME, HOLY SPIRIT

LONGING *to* HEAR
the VOICE *of* GOD

Stormie Omartian has helped millions approach God with confidence and experience His power. With transparency and biblical depth, she now shares what it means to connect with God in a deep and meaningful way through the leading of the Holy Spirit.

Excerpts of the powerful and meaningful prayers from *Lead Me, Holy Spirit* are pulled together for you in this compact book, great for carrying along in a purse, backpack, or briefcase. This is the perfect prayer companion for anyone who desires to know God's Spirit more and grow in a deeper way with Him.

To learn more about Harvest House books and
to read sample chapters, log on to our website:

www.harvesthousepublishers.com

HARVEST HOUSE PUBLISHERS
EUGENE, OREGON